EARTH & SKY

the LAURIE LEWIS SONGBOOK

for Ian & April —
Sing!

CONFLUENCE PRESS

in association with

SPRUCE AND MAPLE MUSIC

Cover photos by Anne Hamersky

Book design by Dan D Shafer
www.dandy-design.com

Published by Confluence Press
Lewis-Clark State College
500 Eighth Avenue
Lewiston, Idaho 83501-2698
(208) 792-2336
www.confluencepress.com
conpress@lcsc.edu

In association with
Spruce and Maple Music
PO Box 9417
Berkeley, CA 94709-0417
www.laurielewis.com
songbook@laurielewis.com

Distributed to the trade by
Midpoint Trade Books
1263 Southwest Boulevard
Kansas City, KS 66103
(913) 831-2233

and 27 West 20th Street, Suite 1102
New York, NY 10011
(212) 727-0190

and 15964 Parklane
Northville, MI 40167
(734) 420-8976

ISBN (paperback): 1-881090-41-8
ISBN (cloth): 1-881090-42-6

TABLE OF CONTENTS

THANK YOU

I owe a deep debt of gratitude to Kathy Kallick, without whose up-close and personal example I might never have begun to write. Thanks also to all the writers, too numerous to mention, whose songs have spoken to me and to whose unknowing tutelage I owe what craft I possess. Among them are: Carol McComb, Tim O'Brien, Mark Simos, Tom Russell, Gillian Welch, David Rawlings, Roy Forbes, Iris DeMent, Walter Hiatt, Hazel Dickens, Jean Ritchie, Sarah Elizabeth Campbell, Jim Mintun, Kate Long, Mark Graham, Richard Thompson, Paul Simon, Hoagy Carmichael, Bruce Cockburn, Carter Stanley, Bob Dylan, Jimmy Martin, Jimmie Rodgers, Merle Haggard, Buck Owens, U. Utah Phillips, Kate Wolf, Hank Williams, Hank Snow, Kitty Wells, Fats Waller, Chuck Berry, John Lennon, Carole King, James Taylor, Don Humphries, Rich Wilbur, Butch Waller, Woody Guthrie and Bill Monroe. A special thanks to Traditional, whose songs and tunes will live forever.

There are many people without whose guidance and work this songbook would never have seen the light of day. My thanks to Stephen Ruffo for insisting that it happen and for persisting in his interest in our progress. Thanks to Tom Rozum for his creative flair, his many great photos, unerring eye and invaluable assistance. Thanks to all the photographers who allowed us to reproduce their photos here and to the unknown photographers who have shared their pictures with me through the years. Thanks to Scott Nygaard and Eric Crystal for their great and careful ears in transferring my tunes to the written page, and to Daniel Steinberg for checking them. Thanks to all the interested parties who wrote urging us forward. Thanks to Bob Rigel and KC Groves for taking this project one step further; to Nigel Renton for his editorial skill; and to Dan Shafer for final design and unflagging attention to detail. And finally, I must thank Jim Hepworth, my publisher, for his great enthusiasm and for shepherding this book through the presses and out into the world.

COURTING THE MUSE *from "Sing Out!" magazine*

I write in fits and starts. Months of apparent inactivity give way to periods of intense productivity. I used to think that, during the dry spells, the muse had gone away for good and I'd never write again. Now I see these times as continuing to create on a different, not so obvious, level. If I live consciously in the world, cognizant of my reactions and emotions and the reactions and emotions of those around me, then I'm working on the next round of songs.

I keep a folder with scraps of paper in it (all kinds: restaurant napkins, old receipts, backs of flyers, and actual notebook pages) on which are scribbled lines, ideas, a verse or chorus, emotional rants, interesting facts, and things attempting to be poems. I carry it around with me everywhere when I'm on a writing jag, and read and reread the snippets with guitar in hand, trying out grooves and melodies until something starts to gel. The folder is really important to me because often I come up with the start of a song and am unable to continue with it, either because of time constraints, or an intellectual or emotional unreadiness to tackle the subject, or just plain stuckness. And because I'm not disciplined enough to have a notebook or tape recorder with me always, I need one place where everything goes.

Creativity for me takes time and, usually, effort. There is the occasional song that seems to just be transmitted through me, like automatic writing. These songs are certainly like some kind of magic, but aren't always my best work. Some songs I labor over for years, unwilling or unable to commit to completion. I do lots of editing, trying to make the lines flow and make each word necessary, and not repeat my chordal and melodic ideas over and over again. To escape that pitfall, I listen to other music. My main inspirations come from roots: early bluegrass, jazz, Mexican, Celtic ballads, all kinds of country, blues, soul. If I'm stuck with a lyric and no framework for it, I'll often just immerse myself in whatever vague idea for a groove I might have and try to open my ears to other possibilities.

A major source of inspiration for me comes from reading. I love the poetry of language, the rhythm and imagery of great writers. I'm almost always in the middle of a novel. Books enrich my vocabulary, enlarge my world view, and take me out of myself. And they are like little mini-vacations. I highly recommend giving yourself the time and permission to read fiction. It's more involving, fun and useful than most self-help books or magazine articles.

A main ingredient in my creative process is solitude. I need time and space and silence to hear myself think, to empty my head of all the logistics problems and chores of my days. I do much of my best thinking while walking or riding my bike. It's not like real, concrete sentences — just centering and being in the (non-anthropocentric) world. My schedule tends to be very hectic: lots of traveling, and time on the phone when I'm at home. When I'm ready to plunge into a new batch of songs it often works to just schedule a retreat somewhere — a place where the phone doesn't ring (at least not for me) — and set myself to the task of taking all my bits of inspiration and completing the songs. I have to admit that deadlines can be very helpful. Some of my best songs have come out of the need to have one more of a certain groove for a recording project.

I haven't done very much co-writing, tending to be overly-protective of the frail little beginnings of my songs. And I don't like being told what I can and can't do. A certain Nashvillian told me once that I couldn't use the word "proximity" in a country song, and that was the end of that partnership (of course, I still haven't finished the song in question). However, when the shared process of creating works its best, you get that hybrid vigor, that something that neither party would have come up with on their own. Someone you trust emotionally and respect musically and who can be objective, open-minded and intuitive would be the ideal collaborator. When you find one, don't blow it.

Ultimately, there comes the time to put pen to paper. I keep in mind a quote from E. M. Forster: "How do I know what I think until I see what I say?" It's the physical writing down that opens the doors of the heart and lets the mind wander in. I prefer writing to typing, both because I'm better at it and for the physicality of it. I like the way the ink leaves the pen. I like that the first draft stays there; nothing can be deleted, just crossed out and usually still legible. And you never know when a line tossed out of one song might be the seed of another.

NOTES ON THE NOTES

In these transcriptions, we have tried to capture the bare bones melody of each song. For ease of reading, we have left out much of the vocal ornamentation and syncopation in the phrasing. It is recommended that you refer to the recording if you need help getting the feel of the music. The songs are for the most part written in the keys in which they were recorded.

This by no means indicates that these are the keys in which they should be sung. That is up to the individual singer, entirely. Chords are provided in the notation. In addition, each song has notes on guitar capoing and chord position in which it was recorded. Chords in the capoed position are provided in parentheses.

SONGS

the LAURIE LEWIS SONGBOOK

ANGEL ON HIS SHOULDER

A true story as told to me and through me.

Words and music by Laurie Lewis
Spruce and Maple Music / ASCAP

VERSE TWO:

He's got an angel on his shoulder

And it guides him through tough times

He didn't always know it

But now he sees it shine

Time was he was too blind to see

So it took him by surprise

When one day it up and spoke to him

And the scales fell from his eyes

And though he may be far from loving arms

He's never all alone

He's got a space upon his shoulder

That an angel calls its home

VERSE THREE:

There was a wreck upon the highway

And as the van began to roll

His angel said, "I'm right beside you

It's ok, man, just let go"

And in the midst of a waking nightmare

He had the calming feel

Of cool wings wrapped around him

And it was just as real

As the shattered glass, the blood and grit

The high, shrill siren's squeal

And he knew he'd beat the odds

Of what was given in that deal

VERSE FOUR:

He says all of his adversities

Just open up his eyes

To all of life's sweet blessings

Spread like stars across the skies

Or dewdrops snared on spider's webs

In an early morning field

It's a picture he can hold to

It protects him like a shield

He's got an angel on his shoulder

And if I'm still it seems

That I feel a slight wind stirring

And I hear the noise of wings

Barbara Karol

Grant Street band, Solana Beach, California, 1996.
Back to front: Paul Knight, Peter McLaughlin, Jerry Logan,
Tom Rozum, and Laurie.

BANE AND BALM

Over the years I've learned to be more guarded with my heart, to sense dangerous entanglements more quickly and to pull back to some kind of safety. But who was it who said, "If you're not living life on the edge, you're taking up too much space"?

Words and music by Laurie Lewis
Spruce and Maple Music / ASCAP

Refrain

Bane — and balm — to my soul —

An - gel be - dev -il -ing me — You taunt — and then-

— con - sole — With a love that can - not

be — *Fine*

Verse

You tell me ev -ery thing will work out — You tell me

we'll be fine — So tell me how to let — this

hurt — out — Tell — me I won't — lose — my mind —

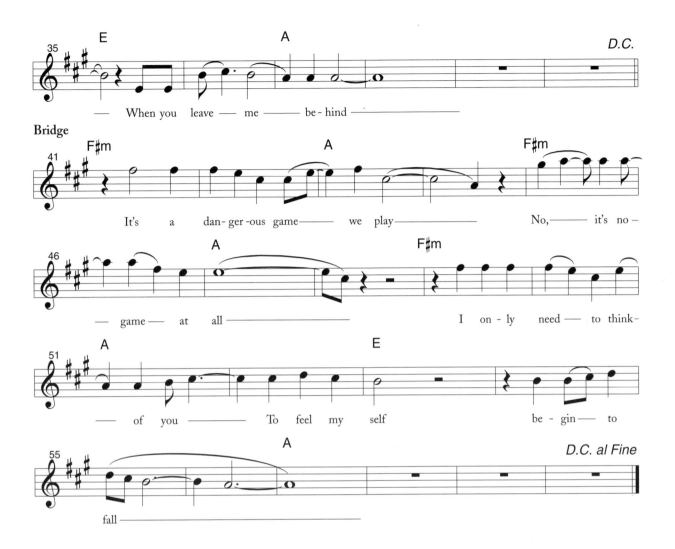

When you leave — me — be-hind

Bridge

It's a dan-ger-ous game — we play — No, — it's no —

— game — at all — I on-ly need — to think-

— of you — To feel my self be-gin — to

fall —

VERSE TWO:

The trick is I have to find

Someone who won't make me think of you

But that requires some sleight of mind

I'm just not quick enough to do,

Or maybe I don't want to

CHORUS

VERSE THREE:

I think my heart's in danger

You think I think too much

You say it'll be okay

But there's danger in your touch

VERSE FOUR:

There's danger in your touch

In the way you speak my name

There's danger in your eye

Oh, it's a dangerous game

And I swear you feel the same

BRIDGE *(written above)*

CHORUS

THE BEAR SONG

I grew up with a copy of Joaquin Miller's True Bear Stories, *which was my father's when he was a kid. One of the tales in that collection and a remarkable visitation by a dream bear following a viewing of Kurosawa's Dersu Uzala were the inspirations for this one, originally recorded in 1983 with the Grant Street String Band. "The big bear in the middle" was Tom Rozum's model for his popular Grant Street t-shirts.*

Words and music by Laurie Lewis
Spruce and Maple Music / ASCAP

Intro/Instrumental Bridge A

Verse

Well, far a-way in the north— coun-try there lived a fid-dl-er fair,— The towns-folk called— him "Moon— Mad John," a bro-ther to the bear.

Instrumental Bridge B

Fiddle Tune:

Musical Note: The ╱ indicates that the note slides upward toward the next half-step of the scale.

VERSE TWO:

Now, Moon Mad John has a tale to tell
To all who'll set a while.
The children listen eagerly
While the grown-ups only smile.

VERSE THREE:

Was in the winter of '25
I was checkin' my traps one day,
When a storm come howlin' from the north
And I did lose my way.

VERSE FOUR:

Well, I soon was cold and hungry
And the darkness did come down.
I knew my death was closin' in
And the wolves were howlin' round.

VERSE FIVE:

So I wandered 'round as in a daze
And I fell down on the ground.
I don't know how long I lay there
When I was wakened by a sound.

VERSE SIX:

Oh, through the trees I peered
(May lightning strike if I'm a liar)
I saw big shadows movin' slow
In the flickerin' of a fire.

VERSE SEVEN:

Well, the bears were all a-gathered there
Dancin' and playin' fiddles.
And the finest fiddler I ever did see
Was the big bear in the middle.

Continued on next page...

VERSE EIGHT:

They took me in and they sat me down
And the fire did thaw my feet.
They gave me food and wine to drink
And soon I fell asleep.

VERSE NINE:

When I awoke next mornin'
The day was clear and bright.
The snow lay trampled all about
But there was not a bear in sight.

VERSE TEN:

So, three days south I traveled
'Til I come to my own front door.
I threw all my guns and my traps away
And I never did hunt no more.

VERSE ELEVEN:

And now you've heard my story
And here for proof's the tune
That the bears did play when they saved my life
Under the winter moon.

Harry Yaglijian

Grant Street String Band, Berkeley, California, 1979.
Left to right: Brian Godchaux, Laurie, Candy Godchaux, Stan Miller, Steve Krouse, Greg Townsend, and Beth Weil.
Front : Angelina Godchaux and Shep.

California Bears On the Front Range

T-shirt design for Grant Street featuring
the "big bear in the middle" and other
Tom Rozum artwork used on Grant
Street flyers.

BLOW, BIG WIND

Sometimes, the only way to help a relationship is to just leave. And it can be so hard.

Words and music by Laurie Lewis
Spruce and Maple Music / ASCAP

Verse

Since you first claimed — my heart — I've been starved for un-der-stand-ing So I plan-ted a gar-den where none — grew be-fore — But the seeds — would not take hold — in this harsh and bar-ren land — — and the on-ly peace I've found — was in the eye — of the storm —

Refrain

So blow, — big — wind — like a storm — on the sea — Blow — big — wind — you

Musical Note: ⌐ indicates a yodeled note

California Bears On the Front Range

LAURIE LEWIS & GRANT STREET
Berkeley, CA

T-shirt design for Grant Street featuring the "big bear in the middle" and other Tom Rozum artwork used on Grant Street flyers.

BLOW, BIG WIND

Sometimes, the only way to help a relationship is to just leave. And it can be so hard.

Words and music by Laurie Lewis
Spruce and Maple Music / ASCAP

Musical Note: ♪ indicates a yodeled note

can't ———————— shake me ——————————

VERSE TWO:

I guess I've been an optimist, or maybe just a fool

To think that these storms would ever cease

I just craved your touch and though the summers were short

They'd always bring sweet release

CHORUS

VERSE THREE:

Now I've pulled up my stakes and packed up my bags

And though I can't stop my heart from this grieving

When the next storm comes rolling in it won't catch me

'Cause everything's over but the leaving

CHORUS

Laurie and Mary Gibbons, San Francisco, California, 2000.

Blue Days, Sleepless Nights

Some cloudy nights I just can't seem to find that guiding star. It's important to keep recharting the course.

Guitar Notes: Played out of E position, capoed on third fret.
Capoed chords shown in parentheses.

Words and music by Laurie Lewis
Spruce and Maple Music / ASCAP

VERSE THREE:

I used to dance out on the edge

I was possessed, I could not fall

Nowadays, I just inch along this ledge

Afraid to dance, I barely crawl

CHORUS

VERSE FOUR:

Many times I have mistaken

The light in another's eye for my own

Just to be led astray again

With no light of my own to guide me home

CHORUS

REPEAT VERSE ONE

Clark and Hazel

I wrote this on the occasion of the fiftieth wedding anniversary of my friends, Clark and Hazel DeLozier. It's a rare and wonderful thing to witness a relationship in which mutual respect and love have flourished over a lifetime together.

Words and music by Laurie Lewis
Spruce and Maple Music / ASCAP

Verse 1

The years ——— they seem to roll ——— by and though we're nei-ther one quite—— so —— spry ——— as on that day so —— long a-go ——— you first took my hand——— and held me close Still, if I—— were asked—— to choose ——— one man a-lone——— for my cap-tain and crew I—— would-n't hes-i-tate,—— no I would choose —— you ————————

Chorus 1

lead- So dance ——————— with your arm —— round —— my —— waist ———

Continued on next page...

Chorus 2

So dance— with your hand— hold - ing mine—

— we'll go round— and — round —

as our lives in - ter — twine —

Anne Hamersky photographing Clark and Hazel DeLozier in 1996, holding a photo of themselves from 1937.

Laurie Lewis

Instructors, Bluegrass Week,
Augusta Heritage Center,
Elkins, West Virginia, 1995
Left to right: Lynn Morris,
Ronnie Simpkins, Laurie,
and Dudley Connell.

Postcard by Tom Rozum, 1998.

Charles Sawtelle and Laurie, Denver, Colorado.

COWGIRL'S SONG

*The Cowgirl's Song was made up to keep myself awake while traveling across Nevada. Not an easy feat. I have to admit that originally I wrote it as the **Cowboy's Song**, but an ever-vigilant feminist male friend pointed out the error of my ways.*

Guitar Notes: Played out of G position, capoed on second fret.
Capoed chords shown in parentheses.

Words and music by Laurie Lewis
Spruce and Maple Music / ASCAP

Verse

Rid - in' a - long with my hat thrown back, ——— my po - ny's bri - dle is a - jing - lin' a tune, ——— and when night-time is fal - lin' and the night owl is cal - lin', we'll be mak - in' our camp by the light of the moon. ———

Refrain

Tum - ble - weeds blow - in' and sage - brush is grow - in' spread-ing its scent ——— through the soft sum - mer breeze ——— and my old pin - to po - ny is my on - ly com - pan - ion as we ride the wide

Musical Note: ♪ indicates a yodeled note

Continued on next page...

Sometimes we gallop across the wide prairies

Laughing and singing with no reason why

And then sometimes at night when the moon's shining bright

I'm as lonesome and blue as a coyote's cry

REFRAIN

VERSE THREE:

When Fall comes on us we round up the mavericks—

They're skittish and quick as a prairie dog's tail—

And then we haze the herd south to weather the winter

To weather a winter of snowstorms and hail

REFRAIN

Mike Stevens

Tom Rozum and Laurie, Alpine, Texas, 1993.

National Old-Time Fiddle Festival, Weiser, Idaho, 1973. Official photo of 5th Place winner, Ladies' Division.

Laurie with Todd Phillips, Mohican Bluegrass Festival, Ohio, 1996.

DON'T GET TOO CLOSE

I remember sitting on my front porch in January, experiencing the strange sensation of a warm south wind. It was so unexpected, so pleasant a change from the cold, damp north winds we'd been having, and also not to be trusted. The kind of weather that makes the trees start pushing out blossoms way too early. And contemplating the weather led me naturally to contemplating love and the fact that it can be so damned inconvenient sometimes. Originally I started writing the first verse about south winds in January, but December is just so much easier to sing and rhymes so nicely. Because the song was written with a band in mind, I didn't feel it needed to be any longer, leaving plenty of room for everyone to play the tune.

Words and music by Laurie Lewis
Spruce and Maple Music / ASCAP

lieve —— to my soul —— that I —— be-gan to re-mem - ber ——

fee - lings that — I thought— were dead— and bur-ied long a - go ——————

REFRAIN

VERSE TWO:

I guess I'd grown accustomed to the cold

I'd bundled up my dreams and pulled my heart inside

I didn't realize — I thought it part of growing old

But here are all these feelings flowing like a spring tide

REFRAIN

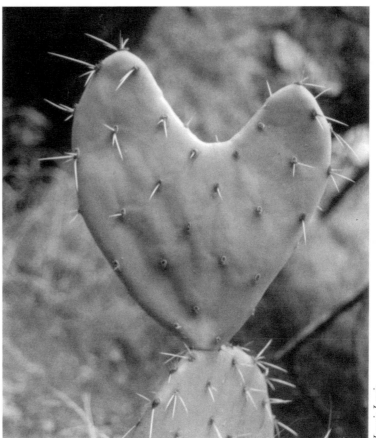

Cactus heart, Zion National Park.

FINE LINE

It's difficult to withhold judgement, but I try to look at all sides of a situation and to always keep in mind that I'm not inside the other person's head.

Guitar Notes: Played out of E position, capoed on first fret.
Capoed chords shown in parentheses.

Words and music by Laurie Lewis
Spruce and Maple Music / ASCAP

Refrain

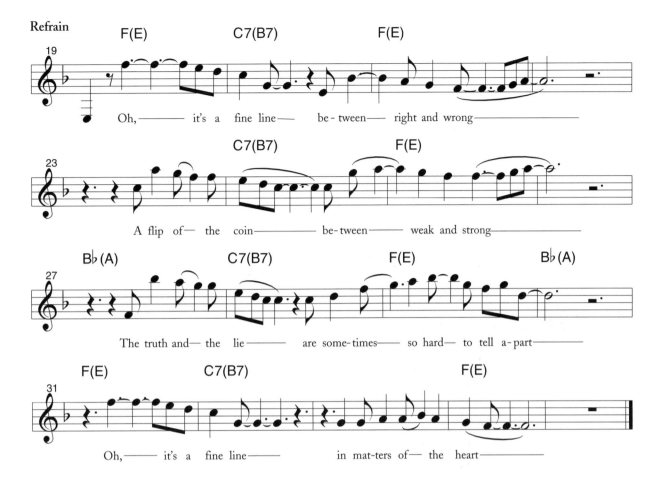

Oh, ——— it's a fine line ——— be-tween ——— right and wrong ———

A flip of— the coin ——— be-tween ——— weak and strong ———

The truth and— the lie ——— are some-times— so hard— to tell a-part———

Oh,——— it's a fine line——— in mat-ters of— the heart———

VERSE TWO:

You say that she's grown cold, she doesn't love you anymore

You say, except for the kids, you'd be out that door

You say you've found someone new, you're afraid you'll lose your heart

But you won't give it up, now that you've let it start

VERSE THREE:

She says that you've grown cold, you don't love her anymore

She says you two used to laugh, now it's just silent chores

She says you turned her away, and so she turned to her friends

She doesn't need you anymore, and so the story ends

REFRAIN

Laurie's mom, Barbara
Moen Renton, ca. 1946.

Laurie's dad, Louis W. Lewis, ca. 1943.

Louis Lewis (the piccolo player on the left), in the MGM
movie "There's Magic in Music," 1940.

Gumbo, Grits, and Gravy tour, 1999.
Left to right: Kevin Wimmer, Courtney Granger, Mark Schatz, Tom Rozum,
Guy Davis, Laurie, Christine Balfa, Craig Smith, and Dirk Powell

"Our Ass Is Grass," Bluegrass Pals promo card (an old postcard doctored by Tom Rozum,) 2000.
Left to right: Tom Rozum, Mary Gibbons, Laurie, Craig Smith, and Todd Phillips.

GIRLFRIEND, GUARD YOUR HEART

Just a friendly little piece of advice: he really is Prince Charming, and we really do feel just like Sleeping Beauties. It's just that the last page of his book is missing.

Guitar Notes: Played out of E position, capoed on third fret.
Capoed chords shown in parentheses.

Words and music by Laurie Lewis
Spruce and Maple Music / ASCAP

VERSE TWO:

He's got a talent for the thing he does

Because he truly believes in the buzz

And with his guileless eyes he'll swear you're the one

But he'll be looking for a bigger kick when the rush is gone

CHORUS, BRIDGE, CHORUS

GREEN FIELDS

I spent my "formative years" running wild in Michigan. Although my older sister informs me that it was the suburbs, I remember it vividly as being only a block away from the country. On a return trip some years later, it had all been swallowed up by a vast sprawling city. I prefer my memories.

Guitar Notes: Played out of C position, capoed on second fret.
Capoed chords shown in parentheses.

Words and music by Laurie Lewis
Spruce and Maple Music / ASCAP

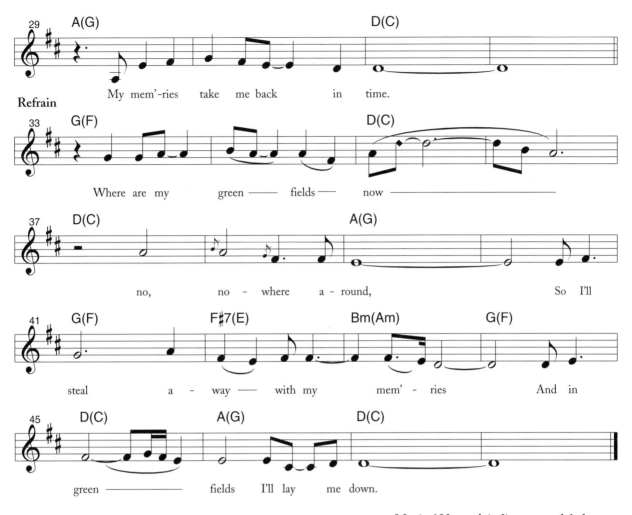

My mem'-ries take me back in time.

Refrain

Where are my green ——— fields ——— now ———

no, no - where a - round, So I'll

steal a - way ——— with my mem' - ries And in

green ——— fields I'll lay me down.

Musical Note: 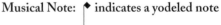 indicates a yodeled note

VERSE THREE:

Now I've got concrete for my front yard
and it's the same way out back
But still it fills my heart with happiness
To see green grass push through the cracks

REFRAIN

VERSE FOUR:

I guess I share the same time-worn dream
with folks in cities everywhere
To find a little place on God's green earth
And live in peace and quiet there

REFRAIN

Laurie and friend, Ann Arbor, Michigan, 1955.

HAVEN OF MERCY

It's hard to accept loss as a part of life. This is my testimonial to the healing powers of the natural world. Specifically, it's a small outcropping of rock somewhere between Anchor Bay and Point Arena above the Mendocino coast.

Guitar Notes: Played out of G position, capoed on third fret.
Capoed chords shown in parentheses.

Words and music by Laurie Lewis
Spruce and Maple Music / ASCAP

Continued on next page…

The hawk hangs above me, the raven flies below,

The quail has found a hiding place in the woods so dark and low.

And I'm like a tiny sparrow that's found a place to nest

At the very gates of heaven — my haven of rest.

REFRAIN

At home in the kitchen gluing the top back on a fiddle, 1996.

Tom Rozum

Fiddle fest on the dining room table.

Laurie Lewis

HERE COMES THE RAIN

Written at the end of a seven-year drought in California. I've noticed that Westerners seem to appreciate the song more than Pennsylvanians do.

Words and music by Laurie Lewis
Spruce and Maple Music / ASCAP

Verse

I've been wai-ting for so long, I've been list'-ning for your song —

I've been scan-ning the skies, sear-ching for clouds — on the hor-i-

zon and here they — come. — And I know — you're go-ing to fall —

— to the thir-sty earth a-gain Here comes — the rain. —

Refrain

Here comes — the rain. —

Here comes — the rain. —

Bridge I

Ev-er-y day — no-thin' but blue — skies —

Earth— is cracked   Fields are tin-der dry —

Bridge II

My heart's — a-bout— to burst— like these clouds ——————— I've been

so — long——— thirst - y, — but it's al-most o - ver now ——— The

first few drops just raise — the dust, The next few drops re - store my — trust Like a

lo - ving hand — can ease — the pain   Here   comes the rain

VERSE TWO:

The tired and dusty trees lift their crowns of withered leaves

They know what's going to come

And that soon the rain will be drumming on the ground

They can feel it in the breeze—oh, it's been a long time gone

And here it comes

REFRAIN, BRIDGE I

VERSE THREE:

It's been silent as death, I've been holding my breath

Now you've returned

Only you can quench this burning in my chest

I need a cold and icy touch, I just can't get enough

Here comes the rain

BRIDGE II, REFRAIN

Tom Rozum

THE HILLS OF MY HOME

My heart quickens when the Coast Range comes in view. Those green and tawny hills are disappearing under housing developments at an alarming rate, making the semi-wild regional parks in the East Bay all the more precious and necessary. This is my ode to Tilden Park.

Guitar Notes: Played out of G position, capoed on third fret.
Capoed chords shown in parentheses.

Words and music by Laurie Lewis
Spruce and Maple Music / ASCAP

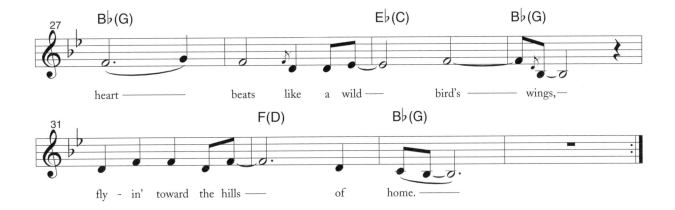

heart ——— beats like a wild ——— bird's ——— wings,—

fly - in' toward the hills ——— of home. ———

VERSE TWO:

Like the sheltering wings of an old mother hen

The hills hover 'round me and my hurts start to mend

And resting on those sunny slopes I truly understand

What it's like to be held in the palm of God's hand

REFRAIN

VERSE THREE:

I'd like to grow old with the grace of an oak

Where the poppies and the lupines and the wild iris grow,

And when I die, good people, grant one last request:

Lay me down beneath the hills that I love best

REFRAIN

The Good Ol' Persons, 1974.
Left to right: Laurie, Sue Shelasky Walters, Kathy Kallick,
Dorothy Baxter, and Barbara Mendelsohn.

I Don't Know Why

This is the first song I wrote, or maybe I should say the first song I ever finished. I was heavily influenced at the time by Buck Owens and the Bakersfield sound. My heart skips a beat when I hear Buck and Don Rich sing together!

Words and music by Laurie Lewis
Spruce and Maple Music / ASCAP

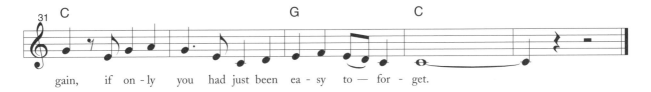

gain, if on-ly you had just been ea-sy to — for-get.

REFRAIN

VERSE TWO:

I guess I've got the strength to leave
But I have no strength to stay away
And the battles that we fought, dear
They're the same we'd face today.
The sight of you brings back to mind
All the wounds upon my heart —
I can't live with you, but, my darlin'
I'm afraid to live apart.

REFRAIN

Laurie, Craig Smith and Tom Rozum in a photo booth at the Space Needle, Seattle, Washington, 1987.

Laurie, Sam Bush, Nick Forster (obscured) and John Cowan, Zlin, Czechoslovakia, 1990.

I'd Be Lost Without You

From the mid-'70s through the mid-'80s, I often played bass and sang with Dick Oxtot's Golden Age Jazz Band. The sounds have gotten in my head and fused (gotten confused?) with country music.

Words and music by Laurie Lewis
Spruce and Maple Music / ASCAP

I'll Take Back My Heart

I used to love to listen to the Norteño music that played on the radio up and down the San Joaquin Valley. That Ranchero sound is what I tried to capture in the feel of this song. Special thanks go to Chris Strachwitz for enriching my life.

Words by Laurie Lewis and Jerry Logan
Music by Laurie Lewis
Spruce and Maple Music / ASCAP

Oh ———— ba-by — don't———— hide.————

Well, ——————— I know ——————— it can

hurt so — some-times———— to let go.———— When times–

———— get hard ———— you know I won-der why— I try. ———— But then

just to see you smile———— makes the sun - shine in my sky.————

Dar-lin' you know that it's— true ————

I'd ———— be lost———— with-out———— you.————

I'll Take Back My Heart

I used to love to listen to the Norteño music that played on the radio up and down the San Joaquin Valley. That Ranchero sound is what I tried to capture in the feel of this song. Special thanks go to Chris Strachwitz for enriching my life.

Words by Laurie Lewis and Jerry Logan
Music by Laurie Lewis
Spruce and Maple Music / ASCAP

Verse

I'll take back my heart

you can't use it any more

I'll put it away

and lock up the door

I'll take back my heart

and set myself free

When it comes down to it

you know it's all —— up to me ——

Refrain

I can't take back the tears, ——

they've all —— dried —— and gone ——

I can't take back the years ——

I've got to move on ——

—— I can't take the dreams ——

they've all —— turned to dust

And blown —— down the road ——

with the love and the trust ——

Continued on next page…

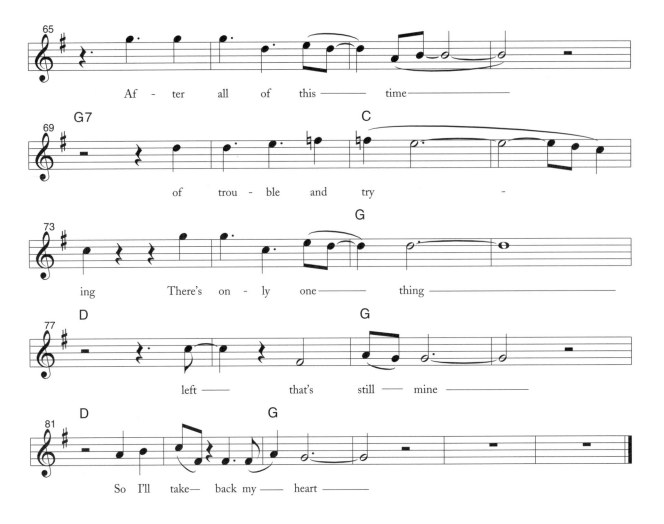

Af - ter all of this —— time —— of trou - ble and try - ing There's on - ly one —— thing —— left —— that's still — mine —— So I'll take— back my — heart ——

VERSE TWO:

It's quite a blow to the pride to be so taken in

By the spark in an eye and the warmth of a grin

Oh, yes, I fanned those flames 'til I got myself burned

So I'll take back my heart — it's a hard lesson learned

REFRAIN

Donut time in Texas, 2001. Tom Rozum, Todd Sickafoose and Laurie.

Sophia, Bulgaria 1990
Left to right: Nick Forster, John Cowan, Sam Bush, and Laurie.

Dick Van Kleeck

Laurie with Tom Rozum and his Iguanatone, Yelapa, Mexico, 1992.

I'm Gonna Be the Wind

This is a statement of intent. I struggle to live up to it every day. Some days I do.

Guitar Notes: Played out of G position, capoed on fourth fret.
Capoed chords shown in parentheses.

Words and music by Laurie Lewis
Spruce and Maple Music / ASCAP

ground,   and I'll fan the flanes of   love,   you know they'll ne-ver   die a -

gain.——— Oh,———   I'm gon-na be   the   wind.

CHORUS

VERSE TWO:

I was waiting, but my name was never called,

And I never tried to stand alone for fear that I might fall—

But now that I'm running, I may never walk again,

Oh, I'm gonna be the wind.

CHORUS

Kenneth Green

Kathy Kallick, Laurie, Barbara Mendelsohn, Paul Shelasky, and Dorothy Baxter,
Bay Records Studio (The Alameda Riddle), Alameda, California, 1975.

Kiss Me Before I Die

Following a disastrous car accident in 1994, I suffered a long drought of creativity. I was incapable of doing anything more than just getting by, working through a long physical and emotional recovery process. People kept making references to the great, deep, meaningful songs that would grow out of the experience. Finally, bent on getting past the block, I went on a retreat, and this song was born. It pretty much says it all.

Words and music by Laurie Lewis
Spruce and Maple Music / ASCAP

VERSE TWO:

While we're just standin' here there could be a quake
We could both be buried alive, so don't hesitate
It may be our last rights we exercise
So come on, pucker up, babe, and let 'er fly
Or on your deathbed you'll have to confide,
"I just wish I'd kissed her before I died"

VERSE THREE:

I think about it every time I fly —
What if this jet were to fall from the sky?
I could slip in the shower and crack my head
Just go to sleep one night and wake up dead
Give me that one thing I'm longing to try
Come on, kiss me before I die

VERSE FOUR:

This is a cry of desperation
I could die of deprivation
It's time to get real, this is not a test
Would you deny a girl her last request?
You know you want it as much as I
Come on, kiss me before I die

Laurie with Ralph Stanley, Masters of the Banjo Tour, Lowell, MA, 1993.

Donna Rae Hirt

Knocking On Your Door Again

I was fooling around on the guitar in an unaccustomed (for me) style and key, and the words eventually took shape around the musical structure. It didn't hurt, I suppose, that I was miserable.

Guitar Notes: Played out of D position, capoed on third fret.
Capoed chords shown in parentheses.

Words and music by Laurie Lewis
Spruce and Maple Music / ASCAP

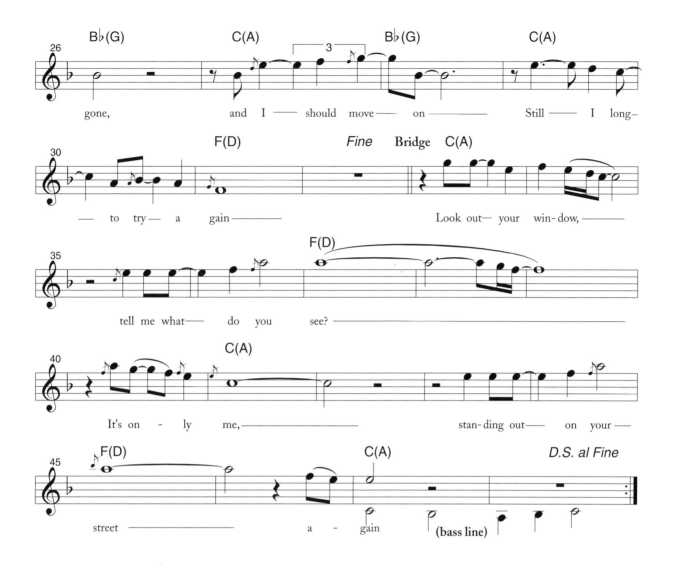

gone, and I — should move — on — Still — I long–

Fine   Bridge

— to try — a gain — Look out— your win-dow, —

tell me what— do you see? —

It's on - ly me, — stan-ding out— on your —

D.S. al Fine

street — a - gain (bass line)

VERSE THREE:

I am here because I can't forget the way you held me near
I can't believe you'd turn away from something so dear
You'd leave me here knocking on your door again

BRIDGE TWO:

I look at your window, I see reflections in the glass
It's only me trying to hold to what's past, and gone

VERSE FOUR:

Here I am, knocking on your door again
One last time, hoping somehow you'll begin
To open your heart, make a new start
Knocking on your door again
I'm knocking on your door again

Laurie with Charles Sawtelle, E-Town radio show,
Boulder, Colorado, 1998.

THE LIGHT

For my grandmother, Hilda Moen. Shortly before she died, she related this experience to my mother.

Guitar Notes: Played out of G position, capoed on second fret.
Capoed chords shown in parentheses.

Words and music by Laurie Lewis
Spruce and Maple Music / ASCAP

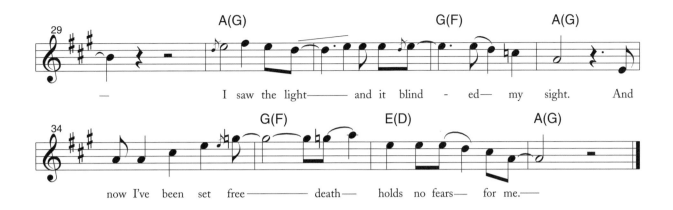

I saw the light———— and it blind - ed— my sight. And

now I've been set free———————— death—— holds no fears— for me.——

VERSE TWO:

I'll miss the sound of thunderstorms

And the sight of the lightning's flash

And I'll miss the scent of sun-warmed earth

And fields of growing grass.

But, oh, most of all,

I'll miss your touch upon my skin.

But be assured, my darling

That we will meet again.

REFRAIN

Grant Street String Band, 1980.
Left to right: Steve Krouse, Beth Weil, Laurie,
Stan Miller (in tree), and Greg Townsend.

Gene Tortora

Lars Bourne

Laurie, Beth Weil, and Rich Wilbur, Fairfield, California, 1980.

LOVE CHOOSES YOU

In my experience, this seems to be true, though there are those who would argue the point. It would be much easier, and safer, if we could just make conscious decisions about such things, but also maybe less wonderful and exciting.

Guitar Notes: Played out of G position, capoed on second fret.
Capoed chords shown in parentheses.
Originally recorded in the key of B.

Words and music by Laurie Lewis
Forerunner Music / Spruce and Maple Music / ASCAP

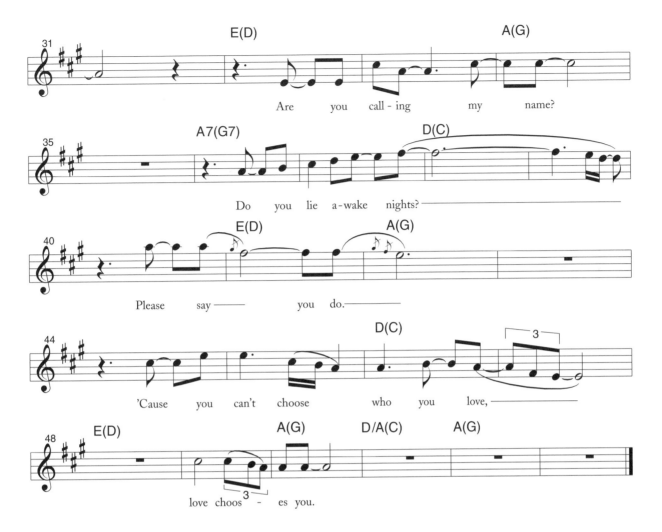

Are you call-ing my name?

Do you lie a-wake nights?

Please say you do.

'Cause you can't choose who you love,

love choos - es you.

VERSE TWO:

In the wink of an eye love looses an arrow;
We control it no more than the flight of the sparrow,
The swell of the tide or the light of the moon.
You can't choose who you love, love chooses you.

REFRAIN

VERSE THREE:

Love cuts like a torch to a heart behind steel,
And though you may hide it, love knows how you feel.
And though you may trespass on the laws of the land,
Your heart has to follow when love takes your hand.

VERSE FOUR:

And it seems we're two people within the same circle;
It's drawn tighter and tighter till you're all that I see.
I'm full and I'm empty and you're pouring through me
Like a warm rain fallin' through the leaves of a tree.

REFRAIN

Halloween Trio: Laurie, Tom Rozum, and
Todd Phillips, Berkeley, California, 1998.

Anne Hamersky

MAGIC LIGHT

I spend a lot of time—too much time—on airplanes. I always try to get a window seat, though, and take advantage of the flight to study geography and geology. By this time I usually know where I am at a glance and can name the major landmarks throughout the lower 48. And every once in a while, Magic happens. This song chronicles about twenty minutes over the Grand Tetons at just the right time. Dedicated to Anne Hamersky, who hunts and captures it on film, and Chuck Forsman, who traps it on occasion with oils on Masonite.

Words by Laurie Lewis
Music by Laurie Lewis and Mike Marshall
Spruce and Maple Music / ASCAP, Rotagilla Music / BMI

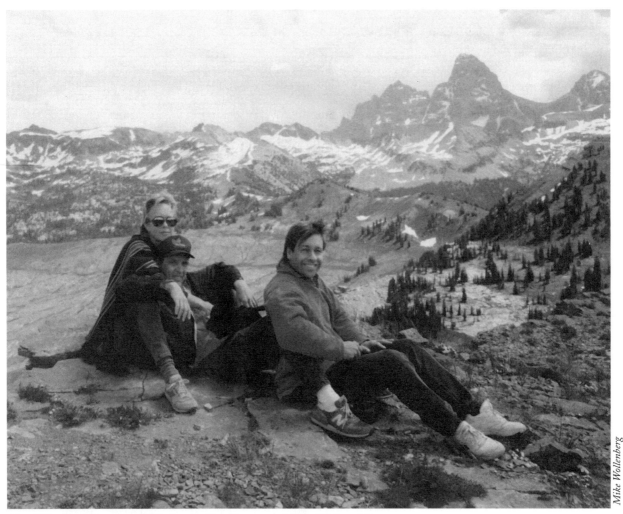

Mike Wollenberg

Grand Targhee, Wyoming, 1994. Laurie, Tom Rozum, and Peter McLaughlin

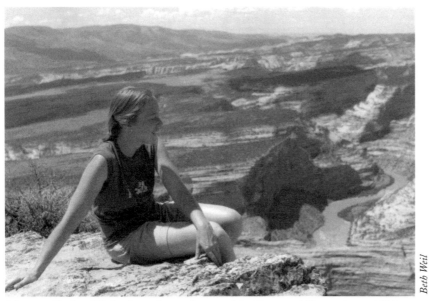

Beth Weil

Dinosaur National Park, above the confluence of the Green and Yampa rivers, 1984.

Tom Rozum

Magic Light, Tilden Park, Berkeley, California, 1995.

THE MAPLE'S LAMENT

From 1981 to 1987 I ran a violin shop. In the beginning, business wasn't great, and I spent many hours surrounded by silent fiddles. It was popular for a time in the 19th century to put a Latin inscription in many violins. The translation, roughly, was something like, "When I was alive I stood mute in the forest. Now, in death, I sing." Well, okay, but what about the tree?

Words and music by Laurie Lewis
Spruce and Maple Music / ASCAP

VERSE TWO:

But now that I am dead, the birds no longer sing in me

And I feel no more the wind and rain as when I was a tree

But bound so tight in wire strings I have no room to grow

And I am but the slave who sings when master draws the bow

VERSE THREE:

But sometimes from my mem'ry I can sing the birds in flight

And I can sing of sweet dark earth and endless starry nights

But oh, my favorite song of all, I truly do believe

Is the song the sunlight sang to me while dancing on my leaves

Hardingfele Solo

Freely

Hardingfele, made by B. Rasmussen in Bergen, Norway, in 1921.

James Wimmer carving the scroll for Laurie's fiddle, 2000.

The hardingfele is a Norwegian folk violin. It has four or five sympathetic strings that run under the fingerboard. Inlay on the fingerboard and tailpiece is shell and bone, in traditional patterns. Decoration on the body is fine brush-work with ink, also in traditional patterns.

THE OAK AND THE LAUREL

A song of lost innocence. Northern California's coastal hills are cut by steep ravines peopled with tough, spiky–leafed live oaks and whispering, aromatic bay laurels.

Words and music by Laurie Lewis
Spruce and Maple Music / ASCAP

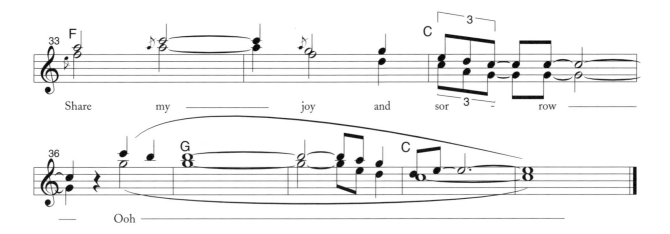

Share my _____ joy and sor — row _____

Ooh _____

VERSE TWO:

The oak, it is a mighty tree, so tall and so strong

And it dares to not bend in the wind

But the laurel has leaves that shiver in each breeze

With their sweet scent, your heart she will win

With their sweet scent, your heart she will win

VERSE THREE:

My love seemed like the oak tree, so tall and so strong

And I thought that his heart would be fair

And his words when he spoke were as sweet in their sound

As the laurel's sweet scent in the air

As the laurel's sweet scent in the air

CHORUS

VERSE FOUR:

The oak and the laurel, they grow side by side

In a valley, down by a clear stream

It was there we parted, my false love and I

And it's there that I'll bury my dreams

It's there that I'll bury my dreams

CHORUS

Laurie and Tom Rozum, official Grammy Nominee photo for "The Oak and the Laurel," 1996.

OLD FRIEND

This song was inspired by a couple of lines written by my old friend, Barbara Mendelsohn. There are a handful of people in my life who have a special hold on my affections that doesn't seem in the least diminished by time or distance. This song is for you —you know who you are.

Words and music by Laurie Lewis
Spruce and Maple Music / ASCAP

With warm — re - gard,———————— and — in — fond a - ffec -

tion I ——— am ——— tru - ly ——— yours ————

VERSE TWO:

Old friend, we've seen so much together

Stormy days and windy weather

And like a cloak against the cold

I wrap myself in friendship's folds

REFRAIN

VERSE THREE:

Old friends like warp and weft entwine

Each crossing defining the design

And though in places frayed and worn

The fabric remains untorn

REFRAIN

Old Friends, 1978. Harry Yaglijian, Laurie, Eric Thompson, Beth Weil, and Gene Tortora.

Harry Yaglijian

THE POINT OF NO RETURN

Isn't it wonderful and scary when you realize what's happening?

Words and music by Laurie Lewis
Spruce and Maple Music / ASCAP

Refrain

Continued on next page…

With the suddenness of Indian summer in the frosty days of fall,

We find we've known each other for such a long time,

And not known each other at all.

And now we're drifting along on an ocean of dreams,

Not thinking that the tide might turn,

And my heart's gone past the point of no return.

REFRAIN

Santa Maria Style Bluegrass Festival, 1991.
Standing, left to right: Alison Brown, Tim Stafford, Audie Blaylock, Adam Steffey, Barry Bales, Tony Furtado, Marshall Willborn, Tom Rozum, Alison Krauss, Lynn Morris, and Scott Nygaard. Kneeling: Tom Adams, Laurie, and Beth Weil.

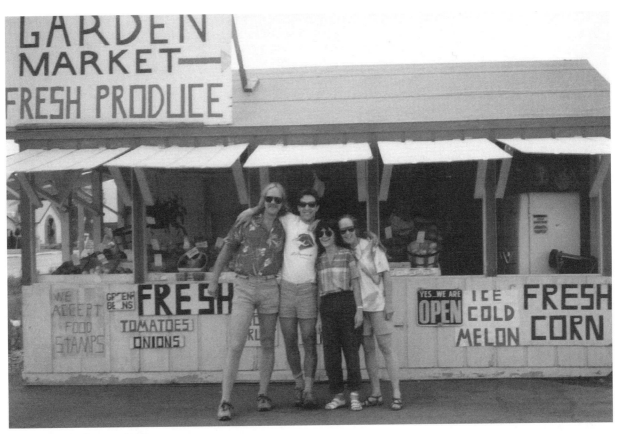

Somewhere in Oregon, 1987.
Left to right: Craig Smith, Tom Rozum, Markie Sanders, and Laurie.

Guitar great George Shuffler and Laurie, Owensboro, Kentucky, 1996.

Sue Shuffler

THE REFUGEE

I thank my lucky stars each night.

Guitar Notes: Played out of G position, capoed on second fret.
Capoed chords shown in parentheses.

Words and music by Laurie Lewis
Spruce and Maple Music / ASCAP

Verse

I'm a tra - veler ⸺ in ⸺ this world ⸺

It's a new town ⸺ ev - ery night ⸺

I've seen ⸺ a lot of coun - try - side

I've mar - veled at the sights ⸺

And I can ⸺ af - ford ⸺ to won - der

at things ⸺ dif - fer - ent and strange ⸺

'cause I have a home ⸺ I ⸺ can - re-turn ⸺ to,

Continued on next page…

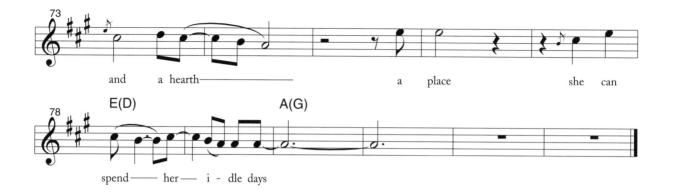

and a hearth ———————— a place she can

E(D)   A(G)

spend ——— her — i - dle days

VERSE TWO:

My family's all around me

And my dear childhood friends

The hills of home surround me

The circle never ends

And I thank my lucky stars each night

And hope I can always say

I've got a home I can return to,

A garden and a hearth,

A place I can spend my idle days

REFRAIN

Grant Street Band flyer, 1989.

Training for the California AIDS Ride
(7 days, 593 miles), 1997.

Laurie, Tammy Fassaert, and Tony Furtado taking a break on the beach,
Pt. Lobos, California, 1989.

RESTLESS RAMBLING HEART

I lived for awhile in an adobe hacienda (stucco apartment) in Corte Madera, California. A sunny day, a little free time, and my beautiful flowering nopales were the inspiration. Also, I think playing for two weeks with Peter Rowan's Free Mexican Airforce had something to do with it...

Guitar Notes: Played out of A position, capoed on third fret.
Capoed chords shown in parentheses.

Words and music by Laurie Lewis
Spruce and Maple Music / ASCAP

hill.——— The moun-tains are cry - in', the prair-ies are sigh - in', and the o-cean is wai - tin' to talk

to me, and my rest - less ram - b-lin' heart — just won't — be still.———

VERSE TWO:

Move a little closer now and hold me tight

I feel like I'm slipping away

I never was quite content just lazin' around

When the birds in the trees are singin' to me

Of places I've never been,

And the road rolling by is calling my name out loud

REFRAIN

Robin Flower, Nancy Vogl,
and Laurie, 1981.

Curly Ray Cline, Ed Neff (obscured) and Laurie, Golden West Bluegrass Festival,
Norco, California, 1975.

THE ROUGHEST ROAD

A song of forgiveness. It's a powerful thing.

Words and music by Laurie Lewis
Spruce and Maple Music / ASCAP

gun_____ I know____ we'll make it through_____

And though____ we stum - ble_____ yet_____ we know

We've al - read - y tra - veled_____

the rough - est road_____ oooh_____ oooh__

_ oooh_____ oooh_____

Fine

VERSE TWO:

The touch of your hand, the warmth of your smile

It's like the first buds of spring, like the laugh of a child

We let fall the armor, let flow the tears

Let go the anger after all of these years

REFRAIN

The Arkansas Sheiks, 1974. Left to right: Tony Marcus, Karana Hattersley, Laurie, and Barbara Mendelsohn.

Sally Van Meter, Laurie, and Kathy Kallick at Paul's Saloon, San Francisco, California, 1981.

Strawberry Music Festival, Camp Mather, California, 1991.
Left to right: Tony Furtado, Tom Rozum, Laurie, Tammy Fassaert, and Scott Nygaard.

Stephen Ruffo

Fiddle class, Bluegrass at the Beach, Nehalem Bay,
Oregon, 1998.

"The Women of Kerrville" tour, Houston, Texas.
Top row, left to right: Nina Gerber, Tish Hinojosa,
Eliza Gilkyson, and Laurie. Kneeling: Anne Hills and
Mary Chapin Carpenter

SAND, WATER AND WAVES

I'm a Californian, what can I say? Though I grieve for her increasing problems — poverty, crime, overpopulation, drought — and always talk about moving, she holds me tight.

Guitar Notes: Played out of A position, capoed on first fret.
Capoed chords shown in parentheses.

Words and music by Laurie Lewis
Spruce and Maple Music / ASCAP

by   sand, ———————— wa - ter,   and   waves ————

VERSE TWO:

The sands keep shifting all the time — the clouds above go rolling by

I'm hypnotized into a trance

And I can only watch the dance,

Sit on the shore of this old bay with sand, water, and waves

REFRAIN

VERSE THREE:

Some few things I'd like to say — but all these little fears get in the way

I feel like life's a grand parade

That I keep trying to evade

So here I'll sit, and here I'll stay with sand, water, and waves

REFRAIN

VERSE FOUR:

Everything is on the move but me — everybody's got some place to be

Some day the tides may shift for me

And pull me out into the sea

But here I'll sit, until that day with sand, water, and waves

REFRAIN

Laurie in the water, 1999.

SEASONS OF THE HEART

Even though this song seems a bit dated (early '80s), I get requests for it all the time. I guess social mores may change, but the human condition remains.

Guitar Notes: Played out of A position, capoed on first fret.
Capoed chords shown in parentheses.

Words and music by Laurie Lewis
Spruce and Maple Music / ASCAP

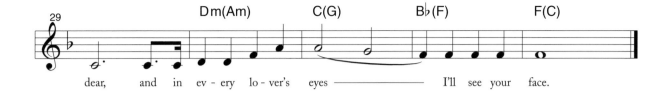

dear,   and   in   ev - ery   lo - ver's   eyes ————————— I'll   see   your   face.

VERSE TWO:

I've heard for everything there is a season,

And I've come to see that winter heralds spring,

So if we have to part I'll try not to regret it,

For the love we shared will brighten everything

REFRAIN

VERSE THREE:

When my last breath on earth is taken,

And all my rivers run down to the sea,

Well, I only hope of me it can be written

That I tried to be the best that I can be

REFRAIN

Carl Fleischbauer

Grant Street String Band rehearsal, Berkeley, California, 1982.
Left to right: Beth Weil, Tom Bekeny, Laurie, Greg Townsend, and Steve Krouse.

SLOW LEARNER

Learning is a life-long occupation. It seems that some people just need more lives than others to figure things out.

Guitar Notes: Played out of G position, capoed on fourth fret.
Capoed chords shown in parentheses.

Words and music by Laurie Lewis
Spruce and Maple Music / ASCAP

VERSE TWO:

So tell me now, is this the way it's always gonna be?

You against the world for all eternity?

You say, "Why don't you trust me?" I say, "Why don't you?

You can't even trust yourself, so what am I to do?"

REFRAIN

SO BEAUTIFUL

Jazz trumpet player Jack Minger gave me a tape of this lovely composition shortly before I left on a European tour. He said, "Maybe I shouldn't tell you this — it may color the way you hear the tune — but I wrote it for my dog, Babe. She was a Great Dane, and when she died, I just sat at the piano and wrote this tune for her. She was just so beautiful." I filed that away in my mind, listened to the tune, tried several times with no success to write lyrics, and stashed the tape in my suitcase. As fate would have it, the day before I was due to fly home from what was a most grueling tour, I called ahead and received the news that my most constant companion and best friend of ten years — my Australian shepherd mix, Shep — had died. I was devastated, and by the time I got home to my lonely house, I had a non-stop splitting headache and couldn't stop crying. I pulled out Jack's tape and played it over and over again until the words came. It gave some small comfort.

Words by Laurie Lewis
Music by Jack Minger
Spruce and Maple Music / ASCAP

for - get those days, they seem — to me al - ways so beau -

ti - ful, —— and you will al - ways be ————— in —

D.C. al Segno

my me-mo-ry, —— so beau-ti-ful to me —— to me ——

ritard

So beau - ti - ful——— to —— me —————

Laurie and Shep, Corte
Madera, California, 1979.

Steve Pottier

SPINNING SLOW

I try to get out on a river rafting trip at least once a year. I wrote these lyrics while on the middle fork of the Salmon River in Idaho.

Words and music by Laurie Lewis
Spruce and Maple Music / ASCAP

I will go and make my home_____ with the swal___ _____ lows and the swifts _____ a- bove _____ the wild ri - ver ____ where the cur - rent drifts, _____ and I _____ will lose my - self in the shine_____ and__ the slide and the cold__

Continued on next page…

VERSE TWO:

And in the din of voices when
The course is rough and steep
And in the whispered murmur
Where it's still and deep
I will turn my ear
To hear the river's song
And when I've learned the tune
I will sing along

REFRAIN

VERSE THREE:

Where the grand cottonwood stands
And drinks at the water side
Among the sage and pine
I'll watch the river glide
And I will climb a hill
When my time comes to go
And be carried up to heaven
By the eagle and the crow

REFRAIN

Stan Dickson

Tom Rozum, Laurie, Cary Black, and David Grier onstage at the Grand Ole Opry, 1995.

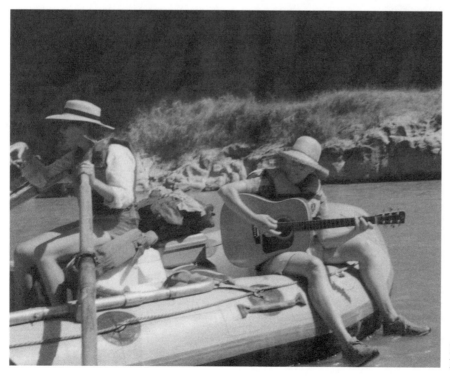

River rafting, Rio Grande,
Big Bend, Texas, 1993.

The Phantoms of the Opry, Mill Valley, California, 1974.
Left to right: Paul Shelasky, Laurie, Gene Tortora, Robbie Macdonald, and Pat Enright.

The Phantoms of the Opry, Paul's Saloon, San Francisco, California, 1975.
Left to right: Laurie, Robbie Macdonald, and Ray Bierl.

SWEPT AWAY

A love that's freely given is never really gone.

Guitar Notes: Played out of G position, capoed on fifth fret.
Capoed chords shown in parentheses.

Words and music by Laurie Lewis
Spruce and Maple Music / ASCAP

Bridge

You were the wind— that brought the clouds and rain——— But now the wind-

— has come to clear my skies —— a-gain — I feel you near— me though I

can-not see your face, and I am swept a-way———————

VERSE TWO:

Oh, the other day I thought I heard you speak my name

Electricity shot through me, but my mind was playing games

And I was swept away

It's just I can't forget you—no, I'm not holding on

For a love that's freely given is never really gone

And I was swept away

Now that it seems that everything reminds me of those days

BRIDGE, REPEAT VERSE ONE

David Grier, Roland White, Laurie, and Tony Trischka, Snoqualmie, Washington.

TATTOO

I had never been overly enamored of tattoos — they're just so damn permanent — until I saw one that really captured my imagination. What can I say? It was perfect! Thanks to M.A. for the inspiration

Words by Laurie Lewis
Music by Mike Marshall and Laurie Lewis
Spruce and Maple Music / ASCAP

swear by the blood — puls - ing through my — veins — This art is sac-red that shapes — your name —

All my life, my lo - ving, my learn-ing, my los-ing, has all —

— been for — this And this a-lone ——— to make me wor-thy of your kiss —

— A - round my arm — in a twis-ted band — of blue I wear — my heart, — your

name, my new tat - too——— Deep — dark — dusk-y blue —

— my — new tat - too ———

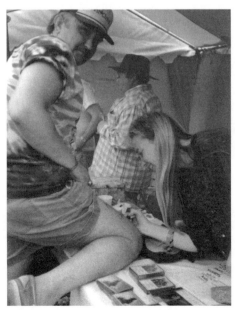

Tattoos while you wait, Winterhawk Bluegrass Festival, Ancram, New York, 1996.

VERSE THREE:

It can't be removed like the ring from a finger

Indelibly printed, it will always linger

It fills me up to always see

A part of you as a part of me

CHORUS

TEXAS BLUEBONNETS

This song was inspired by a beautiful April day spent traveling through central Texas. The song spent the first few years of its life as a waltz and then one fateful day, without warning, rewrote itself under the influence of two of Texas' musical treasures: Bob Wills and Flaco Jimenez. Apologies to the residents of Burnet — I really do know how to pronounce it.

Words and music by Laurie Lewis
Spruce and Maple Music / ASCAP

Tex - as blue - bon - nets would-n't let me for - get.

REFRAIN

VERSE TWO:

I ran out of money, went to work on a farm

Pickin' their melons and hoein' their corn

And all winter long, Lord, I herded their cows

And I tried to forget my little darlin' somehow

VERSE THREE:

But then springtime, it blossomed in every hue

And it just made my heart feel bluer than blue

And those Texas bluebonnets they smiled in the sun

But they just made me think of my only one

REFRAIN

VERSE FOUR:

I'm leavin' the southland, I'm leavin' today

I don't know where I'm going, but I know that I can't stay

I guess I'll go north to the ice and the snow

Where those Texas bluebonnets never will grow

REFRAIN

CODA:

In the cold, frozen north-land I'll live 'til I die

And I'll finally forget my little darlin's blue eyes

American Music Shop, Nashville, Tennessee, 1993.
Left to right: Gene Libbea, Sam Bush, Laurie, and Alan O'Bryant.

Charmaine Lanham

THE TOUCH OF THE MASTER'S HAND

This poem, by Myra Brooks Welch, has been set to music (or something resembling it) many times. Perhaps the most famous version is a dramatic recitation with violin accompaniment by Walter Brennan. It was first brought to my attention by Howard Olivier, who sent me a lovely waltz version. When Kathy Kallick and I started working on our duet album, I needed another uptempo song, so I pirated these oft-pirated lyrics.

Words by Myra Brooks Welch
Music by Laurie Lewis
Spruce and Maple Music / ASCAP

Guitar Notes: Played out of A position, capoed on second fret.
Capoed chords shown in parentheses.

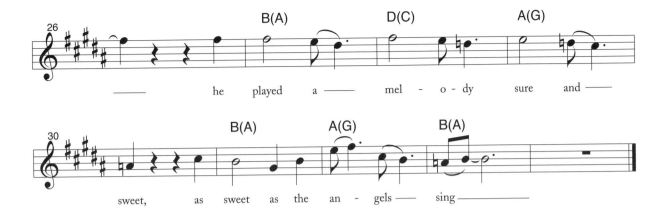

26   B(A)   D(C)   A(G)

____ he played a ____ mel - o - dy sure and ____

30   B(A)   A(G)   B(A)

sweet, as sweet as the an - gels ____ sing ____

VERSE TWO:

"What am I bid, good people?" he said
"Who'll start the bidding for me?
A dollar, a dollar — who'll make it two?
Two dollars — who'll make it three?"

VERSE THREE:

And if it's three dollars once, and it's three dollars twice
And going for three, but no —
From the back of the room a gray-haired man
Came forward and picked up the bow

CHORUS ONE

VERSE FOUR:

The music stopped and the auctioneer,
In a voice that was soft and low,
He said, "What am I bid for this violin?",
And he held it up with the bow

CHORUS TWO:

"A thousand dollars — who'll make it two?
Two thousand — who'll make it three?
And it's three thousand once, and it's three thousand twice,
And going and gone," said he

VERSE FIVE:

The people cheered, but some of them said
"We don't quite understand —
What changed its worth?" and the man replied
" 'Twas the touch of the master's hand"

VERSE SIX:

There's many a man with his life out of tune
And battered and scarred with sin,
Who's auctioned cheap to the thoughtless crowd,
Much like that old violin

CHORUS THREE:

A mess of pottage, a glass of wine,
A game, and he travels on
And he's going once, and he's going twice,
He's going and almost gone

CHORUS FOUR:

And then the Master comes, and the foolish crowd
Can never quite understand
The worth of a soul and the change that is wrought
By the touch of the Master's hand

VAL'S CABIN

For the rivers whose very names fired my childhood imagination, and whose free-flowing waters seemed to me the essence of wildness and beauty: the Stanislaus, Tuolumne, Mokelumne, and Yuba.

Guitar Notes: Played out of A position, capoed on second fret.
Capoed chords shown in parentheses.

Words and music by Laurie Lewis
Spruce and Maple Music / ASCAP

Verse

When I was a kid— and the sum-mers were free — we'd pile in a car— with no— A - C —— and point it east— in-to the heat— A-cross the Cen-tral Val-ley —— We'd drive our ma-ma near— — in-sane,— 'Til she'd pull off — of that big — four lane,— And we— — start-ed up the wind - ing road —— to Val's —— ca - bin ——

Refrain

And the ri - ver runs through all my —— me-mo-ries, —— Twist-ing and plung - ing be - tween the trees,— Slid-ing past great gra-nite boul - ders

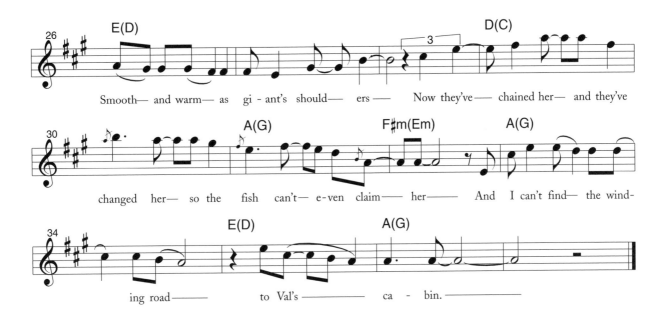

Smooth— and warm— as gi - ant's should— ers — Now they've— chained her— and they've

changed her— so the fish can't e-ven claim— her—— And I can't find— the wind-

ing road——— to Val's——— ca - bin.———

VERSE TWO:

About half-way to the mountain top
We'd pull off the road and come to a stop
By a rustic cabin with the shutters locked
Sure, it was cooler, but still damn hot
But the pine and scotch-broom were in the air
The river was just a few miles from there
Just a ways down the winding road past Val's cabin

REFRAIN

VERSE THREE:

On a long and dusty old dirt track
We'd walk to the river and then trudge back
Stopping to talk to every horse,
Every friendly dog, and every cat
In the water ditch along the road
We'd hide from the sun and dangle our toes;
Then we'd start up the winding road to Val's cabin

REFRAIN

VERSE FOUR:

Now twenty years later I'm climbing that hill
Roaring up the highway past Soulsbyville
It's an oven outside, but it's cool in here
In this air-conditioned automobile
It's four-lane concrete all the way —
They've straightened the curves and smoothed the grades —
They've covered up the winding road to Val's cabin

REFRAIN

Laurie with brother Brian, Gwynn, and Kelly, Val's cabin,
Twain Harte, California, 1965.

Barbara Moen Renton (Laurie's mom)

VISUALIZE

I read a screenplay about a man who kept cutting photos out of magazines and making collages of faces until he came up with the one he was looking for. Then he found her. Convincing her that they were made for each other was a whole 'nother story...

Words and music by Laurie Lewis
Spruce and Maple Music / ASCAP

re - cog - nize ———— the one I'm drea - ming of ——————

Vi - su - al - ize ——————————

Bring ——— me ——— my

love ——————————

D.C.

D.C.

Bridge

Well, I know ———— it's an im - poss - i - ble ro - mance ——

— Like the end of "Ci - ty Lights" —— when she takes — his hand —— And she

looks in - to his eyes —— for the first —— time, and —— she

D.S. al Fine

knows...——————

Continued on next page...

If I just study my heart

Then I could place his smile

Close my eyes

I'll see his profile

Then I will know him

When I hear his voice

On the telephone or across the room

I will know him and I'll see him soon

REFRAIN

Mile 5 of the California AIDS Ride, 1997.

Lonesome Pine Special, Louisville, Kentucky, 1992.
Left to right: Tim Stafford, Scott Nygaard, Cary Black, Alison Krauss, Barry Bales, Laurie, Tom Rozum, and Adam Steffey.

John Fitzgerald

On the set of the Lonesome Pine Special, Louisville, Kentucky, celebrating "Seeing Things," 1998.
Left to right: Billy Lee Lewis, Mike Marshall, Darol Anger, Mary Gibbons, Tom Rozum, Laurie, and Todd Phillips.

Karl Heinz Siber

Laurie, IBMA Female Vocalist of the Year, with Mark Schatz, Bass Player of the Year,
Owensboro, Kentucky, 1994.

THE WIND AT PLAY

This is one of my earliest songs, inspired by the music of Carter and Ralph Stanley and an afternoon on Mt. Tamalpais.

Words and music by Laurie Lewis
Spruce and Maple Music / ASCAP

A field of rape (the plant they make Canola oil from), Germany 1993.
Left to right: Cary Black, Laurie, Scott Nygaard, and Tom Rozum.

VERSE TWO:

This mornin' I woke before dawning
And I cried that we had to part
The sun drove the darkness from the night
And straight into my heart

REFRAIN

VERSE THREE:

At night my room closes around me
My thoughts are all on you,
Darkness presses down on me
Your face is all I view

VERSE FOUR:

Then I long to be on that hillside
The air so bright and clear
I long for the wind to sing for me
And dry my lonely tears

REFRAIN

Flyer from Japan tour, 1996.

THE WOOD THRUSH'S SONG

At Davis and Elkins College in Elkins, West Virginia, there was a beautiful steep wooded gully where I first heard and was captivated by the song of the Eastern wood thrush. This reclusive brown bird is difficult to see, but has the most liquid, lovely voice I think I have ever heard. I read somewhere that some experts believe that it sings so much because it lives in heavy woods with no sight lines, so must keep announcing its whereabouts to its mate. In the name of "progress," the woods were cleared to make way for a new library, and the wood thrush disappeared. I sat on the brick retaining wall and wrote this song.

Words and music by Laurie Lewis
Spruce and Maple Music / ASCAP

oh, how I long to a - gain feel the spell of the wood thru-sh's song.

VERSE TWO:

Over my head just a few years ago
The poplar leaves shivered when the breezes did blow
Now the deep hum of engines drowns the soft sigh
Of the wind in the leaves of the few trees nearby

REFRAIN

VERSE THREE:

Man is the inventor, the builder, the sage
The writer and seeker of truth by the page
But all of his knowledge can never explain
The deep mystery of the wood thrush refrain

REFRAIN

Craig Smith, Tom Rozum, Mary Gibbons, and Laurie, singing "The Wood Thrush's Song," San Francisco, California, 2000.

Charmaine Lambam

Jason Carter, Stuart Duncan, Laurie, Mark O'Connor, and Jerry Douglas,
American Music Shop, Nashville, Tennessee, 1993.

Laurie, Kate Brislin, and Sylvia Herold, Freight and Salvage Coffeehouse, Berkeley, California, 1995.

Laurie with a macaw, Berkeley, California, 1999.

David Grisman, Todd Phillips, Laurie, and Craig Smith,
Bluegrass at the Beach, Nehalem Bay, Oregon, 1999.

You'll Be Leaving Me

Thanks to George Jones, Harlan Howard, and Nashville in general; and to Paul McBride, who told me he'd steal the hook if I didn't use it.

Words and music by Laurie Lewis
Spruce and Maple Music / ASCAP

Verse

When your heart breaks for the first time You know it's not that hard to mend But the hea-ling goes more slow-ly Eve-ry time it breaks a-gain Where once you gave love free-ly Now you're hold-ing it in-side You say you're learn-ing how to live But you're just learn-ing how to hide And that was me, un-til you came a-long You

VERSE TWO:

It seems I just learn how to share my life

When I'm back out on my own

So I learn to not be lonely

Though I find myself alone

And then I'm happy in my own company

When some thief steals my heart

I tell myself, "This is the end,"

But I'm right back at the start

REFRAIN TWO:

And this is it, I'll never give my heart again

You can cry, but darling, this time I won't bend

'Cause I'd find myself needing you and then, too late, I'd see

Just when I'd learn to believe in you, you'd be leaving me

Laurie, Alison Brown, and Doc Watson at MerleFest, Wilkesboro, North Carolina, 2000.

Frank Serio

Todd Phillips, Laurie, Tom Rozum, and Peter McLaughlin, Flagstaff, Arizona, 1997.

Sue Zarske

Paul Shelasky, Laurie, and Sue Shelasky Walters, Paul's Saloon, San Francisco, California, 1975.

Chuck Forsman

Charles Sawtelle and the Bluegrass Imperials, Freight and Salvage Coffeehouse, Berkeley, California, 1995.
Left to right: Tom Rozum, Darol Anger, Laurie, Herb Petersen, Jerry Logan, David Grisman, and Charles Sawtelle.

Jon Sievert

INDEX OF FIRST LINES

DISCOGRAPHY

The following is a list of Laurie's recordings of songs in this book by album.

Grant Street String Band
Bonita Records LP 111, 1983
Reissued on Flat Rock Records, 1997
PO Box 1170, El Cerrito, CA 94530

The Bear Song

Seasons of the Heart

Restless Rambling Heart
Flying Fish FF406, 1986

The Cowgirl's Song

Green Fields

Haven of Mercy

I'm Gonna Be The Wind

The Maple's Lament

Restless Rambling Heart

Love Chooses You
Flying Fish FF487, 1989

Love Chooses You

Texas Bluebonnets

The Point of No Return

I'd Be Lost Without You

Old Friend

The Hills of My Home

I Don't Know Why

The Light

**Laurie Lewis and Grant Street:
Singing My Troubles Away**
Flying Fish FF515, 1990

Don't Get Too Close

**Laurie Lewis and Kathy Kallick:
Together**
Rounder Records 0318

The Touch of the Master's Hand

True Stories
Rounder Records 0300, 1993

Swept Away

Knocking on Your Door Again

Val's Cabin

You'll Be Leaving Me

Here Comes the Rain

So Beautiful

Sand, Water, Waves

Slow Learner

**The Oak and the Laurel:
Laurie Lewis and Tom Rozum**
Rounder Records 0340

The Oak and the Laurel

Clark and Hazel

**Earth and Sky:
Songs of Laurie Lewis**
Rounder Records 0400, 1997

The Bear Song

Don't Get Too Close

Fine Line

Girlfriend, Guard Your Heart

Green Fields

Haven of Mercy

The Hills of my Home

I'd Be Lost Without You

The Light

Love Chooses You

Magic Light

The Maple's Lament

Old Friend

The Point of No Return

Restless Rambling Heart

Texas Bluebonnets

Seeing Things
Rounder Records 0428, 1998

Angel on His Shoulder

Bane and Balm

Blue Days, Sleepless Nights

I'll Take Back My Heart

Kiss Me Before I Die

The Refugee

Tattoo

Visualize

Laurie Lewis and her Bluegrass Pals
Rounder Records 0461, 1999

Blow, Big Wind

Wind at Play

The Wood Thrush's Song

**All Flying Fish and Rounder
titles are available from:**

Rounder Records

One Camp Street

Cambridge, MA 02140

All titles are available from:

Spruce and Maple Music

PO Box 9417

Berkeley, CA 94709-0417

www.laurielewis.com

Spruce and Maple Music